cool cocktails

cool cocktails

Ben Reed photography by William Lingwood

RYLAND
PETERS
& SMALL

London New York

Design Gabriella Le Grazie, Megan
        Smith, Luis Peral-Aranda
Consultant Editor Anne Ryland
Editor Maddalena Bastianelli
Location Research Kate Brunt
Production Patricia Harrington
Art Director Gabriella Le Grazie
Publishing Director Alison Starling

Mixologist Ben Reed
Stylist Helen Trent

First published in the United
Kingdom in 2000
by Ryland Peters & Small
Kirkman House
12-14 Whitfield Street
London
W1T 2RP
www.rylandpeters.com

Text © Ben Reed 2000
Design and photographs ©
Ryland Peters & Small 2000

10 9 8 7 6 5 4 3

Printed and bound in China.

Although all reasonable care has
been taken in the preparation of
this book, neither the publisher
nor the author can accept
responsibility for any
consequences arising from
the use thereof or from the
information contained within.

ISBN 1 84172 079 8

A CIP record for this book
is available from the
British Library.

For Abi, my life companion
and partner in crime and for
my mother Mair, a walking
thesaurus and accomplished
brain-stormer.

contents

Introduction 6

The must-have equipment 10

Mixology techniques 12

Glasses 14

Vodka 16

Gin 42

Whisky 58

Rum 70

Cachaça 86

Brandy, aperitifs & liqueurs 88

Tequila 100

Champagne 108

Non-alcoholic cocktails 116

Hangover cures 122

Index 126

Acknowledgements 128

introduction

The 'cocktail hour' is that special time in the early evening when cocktails always seem particularly appropriate, but of course they can also be absolutely right at any other hour of the day. Between the restorative mid-morning Bloody Mary and the relaxing, late-night Brandy Alexander there are hundreds of great drinks just perfect for the right mood, the right time and the right place.

Mybar at MyHotel

Ever since I discovered the pleasures of making the perfect cocktail to fit the mood, the time and the place, whether for my friends or as a professional bartender, I have been on a mission to tempt people away from the tried and tested onto a more adventurous level of drinking promiscuity.

The classic cocktails still have an important place in the cocktail repertoire but many of them were created during the time when Prohibition was in place and bartenders had a limited range of ingredients at their disposal. Today the variety of spirits, liqueurs and aperitifs is vast, to say nothing of the huge array of mixers and fresh fruit that are available, so it's not surprising that there has been a resurgence of creativity over the past decade and that there is now a wonderful array of tempting drinks for any occasion. Some are modern twists on old classics but many are completely new creations.

the modern cocktail can be tailored to fit the mood of the moment

Modern-day cocktails may be fun or sophisticated, simple or exotic, a pick-me-up or a relaxer, the variety is as infinite as the possible occasions on which to drink them.

No one knows for certain when the cocktail first appeared but it was during the jazz age of the 20th century that it reached its peak of fame. Paradoxically, it was the introduction of Prohibition in the United States during the 1920s that gave birth to the 'cocktail age'. The banning of the sale of alcohol gave rise to a very lucrative trade in smuggled alcohol and later to a well-organized industry of illegal stills. Most of the resulting liquor was dreadful, so using it in cocktails was the only way to make it palatable (as well as being a way of disguising its existence from the police).

Nevertheless, despite this dubious period, the cocktail had found its place in history. It later crossed the Atlantic, where, at the Savoy Hotel in London, it was elevated to the heights of decadent sophistication.

After a period in the doldrums, the popularity of the cocktail has grown again and bartenders have moved it into the new century. The modern-day cocktail can be tailored for those who like to buy bespoke. Whether you are ordering at a bar or mixing drinks for your friends at home, I think you will find plenty of exciting, new ideas here. Cocktails don't have to be complicated – often the simplest ideas work best, especially when the balance of flavours is just right.

I have included cocktails for intimate moments, pre- and after- dinner drinks, glamorous parties and many other occasions, so be adventurous, explore the endless possibilities and have fun.

You will probably find that you already have all the equipment you need to make cocktails in your own kitchen. But if you want to create the right atmosphere for your guests and mix cocktails with a little more style, it's worth getting a few accessories.

the must-have equipment

Measure/Jigger

The first thing any aspiring bartender should acquire is a measure (jigger). Too many professional bartenders regard the jigger as a tool for the novice – their guesswork results in many delicate cocktails being ruined. One of the most inspiring sights of my bartending career was sitting at the Mezzanine Bar at Quaglino's watching the slickest bar team in London as they entertained, served, charmed and consoled the clientele (in that order), measuring every drink, cocktail or otherwise. The useful modern dual-measure jigger measures both 50 ml and 25 ml (a double and a single measure).

Shaker

The shaker is the second most important piece of equipment for a bartender. The Boston shaker, half stainless steel, half glass, is my preference and great for a stylish performance, but the more orthodox shaker with the inbuilt strainer and twist-off cap works equally well.

Barspoon

The barspoon, with its long spiralling handle, is useful for stirring drinks and the gentle pouring required for layered drinks. The 'wrong', flat end can be used for muddling or crushing herbs, etc.

Bartender's Friend

The bartender's friend is a useful implement that removes corks and bottle caps and opens cans.

Muddler

A muddler is a wooden pestle for mixing or crushing sugar cubes, limes and herbs, etc.

Mixing Glass

A mixing glass with strainer is used for making drinks that are stirred, not shaken.

Other useful but not essential accessories are an ice bucket, ice tongs and a citrus squeezer.

mixology
techniques

Creating good cocktails is easy – it's all a matter
of getting the balance of the ingredients just
right and this takes a combination of inspiration,
care and top-quality ingredients.

There are five basic ways of creating a cocktail: building, blending, shaking, stirring over ice and layering. Whichever method you are using, accurately measure the ingredients first to get that all-important balance of tastes right. If you would rather try guesswork just see how much practice it takes to get the quantity right to fill the glass exactly – I still have problems in that department!

Building

The process of building a cocktail just requires adding the measured ingredients to the appropriate glass with ice with perhaps a quick stir before serving.

Blending

This method involves pouring all the ingredients into a blender, adding crushed ice and flicking the switch.

Shaking

Using a shaker is the most enjoyable way to mix a cocktail, both for you and your guests. Add the ingredients to the shaker and fill it with ice. The shaking movement should be sharp and fairly assertive, but do remember to keep your hands on both parts of the shaker or at least a finger on the cap. As an apprentice bartender, I remember neglecting to concentrate whilst entertaining (little was I to know how much!) a group of Australian air stewardesses in a Hong Kong night club and ending up with most of the contents of my shaker of Amaretto Sour and a not inconsiderable amount of egg (white) on my face. Drinks containing egg white, cream and juices should be shaken for slightly longer than the usual ten seconds.

Stirring

This is the best method when you want to retain the clarity and strength of the spirits. Manhattans and martinis, for example, are always stirred. Use an ice-filled mixing glass and stir carefully to avoid chipping the ice and diluting the drink. Frost your serving glasses by leaving them in the freezer for an hour before use.

Layering

A technique used for drinks such as the Pousse Café. With the flat end of a barspoon resting on the surface of the base spirit, pour each of the other spirits in turn down the handle of the spoon. This keeps the ingredients separate and allows them to be tasted separately.

Muddling

Pressing or pounding with the flat end of a barspoon or a muddler mixes or crushes ingredients such as fruit or herbs and allows the flavours to be released gently.

Sugar Syrup

This is easy to make at home. Stir 500 g of sugar into 250 ml of water and bring to the boil, stirring vigorously. Cool and keep in a bottle in the fridge.

A complete range of glasses is not strictly necessary for your cocktail bar in today's more relaxed age. Equip your bar with the essential minimum and use alternatives when required.

glasses

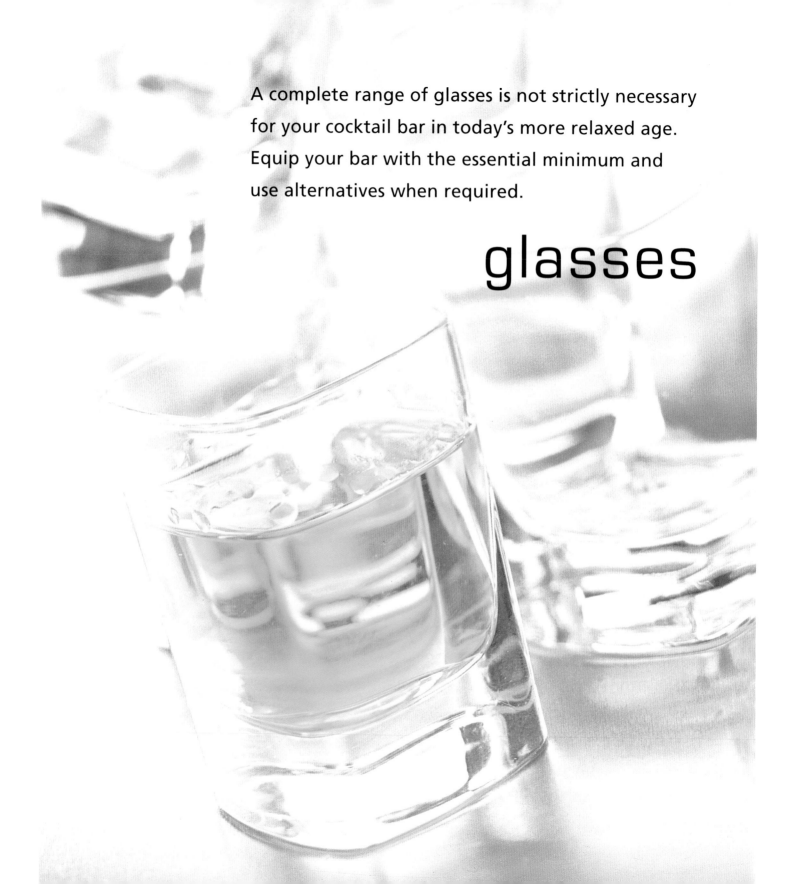

The Martini Glass

The traditional martini glass is a very familar icon. With its open face and slim stem, it epitomizes the elegance essential to any self-respecting martini.

The Cocktail Glass

The cocktail glass is similar to the martini glass but with a slightly rounded bowl, so it's not essential to have both.

The Rocks or Old Fashioned Glass

The rocks or old fashioned glass is similarly purpose-built. It is a squat, straight-sided glass, which sits on a heavy base and feels comfortable in the hand. A drink on the rocks, in a rocks glass, should not be rushed.

The Highball and The Collins

The highball and the collins glasses come in various sizes but they are tall, slim glasses designed to keep a long drink fresh and cold.

The Shot Glass

The small, sturdy shot glass is designed with one purpose in mind: getting what is usually a fairly high-alcohol drink from the glass into one's mouth with as little fuss as possible (and personally I think it does the job very nicely).

The Champagne Flute

The champagne flute is perfect for keeping the sparkle in your champagne cocktails. It should be elegant and long-stemmed with a narrow rim to enhance the delicacy of the drink.

Other useful and versatile, but not essential, glasses are sherry, port, brandy and wine glasses. If you already have them, you can use them as alternatives for some of the above glasses. Another useful glass is a heat-resistant punch or hot toddy glass, which has a stainless steel base and handle.

vodka

Vodka is my favourite spirit, both for its purity and strength drunk neat and as a base for some of the finest cocktails.

To me, vodka has as many flavour permutations as fine wine – from the bitterness of Zubrowka, aromatized with the bison grass that flourishes on the borders between Russia and Poland, to the thick, caramelized sweetness of Goldwasser, a Polish vodka with genuine gold flakes floating in the bottle.

vodka is the strong, silent type at the cocktail bar

It was vodka's flexibility as a cocktail ingredient that first grabbed my attention and it is the base for some of the enduring favourites of the cocktail menu – the Bloody Mary, the Harvey Wallbanger and the Casablanca. However, in the early nineties vodka cocktails took a wrong turn. Bartenders got a little carried away and, with a shocking lack of respect for this wonderful czar of all spirits, began infusing chocolate bars and even jelly beans into some revolting vodka-based cocktails. Thankfully this trend has passed and some of the cocktails created at the Met Bar, including the fresh fruit martini, have saved the reputation of this invaluable spirit.

17

martini

The creation of the 'modern martini' was part of the resurgence of creativity in cocktail making in the mid-1990s that had sadly been absent for many years. The martini became something of a phenomenon in the latter years of the last millennium as it evolved from its original classic form into a whole raft of tempting new tastes. The Polish Martini combines the bitterness of Zubrowka with the potent sweetness of Krupnik and the crispness of apple juice, creating a beguiling depth of taste. The Chocolate Martini was a great discovery, with a dash of white crème de cacao, it saved bartenders from trying to create the chocolate taste by forcing Mars Bars into bottles of vodka! It was the fresh fruit martini, though, that really took London by storm during this period. The Cranilla is the creation of a Met Bar mixologist who combined fresh cranberries with vanilla-flavoured vodka and unwittingly breached the bar's rules of cocktail creation (only fresh produce need apply), but the result was so good we decided to put it on the menu anyway.

polish
martini

25 ml Zubrowka Vodka
25 ml Krupnik Vodka
25 ml fresh apple juice

Add single shots of Krupnik Vodka, Zubrowka Vodka and apple juice into a mixing glass filled with ice. Stir and strain into a frosted martini glass.

50 ml vodka
25 ml crème de cacao (white)
12.5 ml crème de menthe (white)

Into a shaker filled with ice,
pour the vodka, the crème de
cacao and the crème de
menthe.
Shake and strain into a frosted
martini glass with a cocoa rim.

chocolate mint
martini

50 ml Stolichnaya Vanilla Vodka
12.5 ml sugar syrup
a large handful of fresh cranberries

Lightly crush the cranberries
with a barspoon in a shaker. Fill
with ice and add a large shot of
vodka and sugar syrup to taste.
Shake and strain into a frosted
martini glass. Serve with a stem
of fresh cranberries.

cranilla
martini

19

kiwi martini

50 ml vodka
a dash of sugar syrup
1 fresh kiwi fruit

Crush a peeled, sliced ripe kiwi
fruit in a shaker, using a
muddler or the flat end of a
barspoon. Add ice, the measure
of vodka and sugar syrup to
taste. Shake and strain into a
frosted martini glass. Garnish
with a slice of kiwi fruit.

strawberry martini

50 ml vodka
12.5 ml frais de bois (optional)
a dash of sugar syrup
fresh strawberries

Crush three fresh strawberries in
a shaker, using a muddler or the
flat end of a barspoon. Add ice,
a large shot of vodka, a dash of
frais de bois and a hint of sugar
syrup to taste. Shake the
mixture sharply and strain into a
frosted martini glass. Garnish
with a fresh strawberry.

fruit martini

Once London's bartenders discovered that using the juice of ripe, preferably tropical, fruit in cocktails was eminently more desirable than using vodka infused with jelly beans and chocolate, their creativity was unbounded. The fruit used should be as ripe and fresh as possible; the dash of sugar mentioned in the recipes is only to sweeten unripe fruit. Needless to say, when I was making martinis for celebrities at the Cannes Film Festival not a great deal of sugar syrup was used!

watermelon martini

50 ml vodka
a slice of watermelon
a dash of sugar syrup

Put the chopped flesh of the watermelon in a shaker, crush it slightly then add ice, the shot of vodka and a hint of sugar syrup to taste. Shake the mixture sharply and strain into a frosted martini glass. Garnish with a small wedge of watermelon.

metropolitan

This cocktail was one of the originals on the Met Bar menu. It uses one of the more creditable flavours of the vodkas in Absolut's arsenal with great success. The blackcurrant vodka, combined with the cranberry and balanced by the lime juice makes for quite a fruity concoction. It's very difficult to be entirely sure of the origin of any cocktail but I think I can safely claim this one as mine!

50 ml Absolut Kurrant Vodka
25 ml triple sec
25 ml fresh lime juice
25 ml cranberry juice

Shake all the ingredients sharply over ice and strain into a frosted martini glass. Squeeze the oil from a strip of orange zest, skin downwards over a flame, held over the glass. Rub the rim with the orange zest before dropping it into the glass.

a great modern cocktail filled with intense red-fruit flavours

50 ml vodka
a dash of dry vermouth

Fill a mixing glass with ice and stir with a barspoon until the glass is chilled. Tip the water out and top with ice. Add a dash of dry vermouth and continue stirring. Strain the liquid away and top with ice. Add a large measure of vodka and stir in a continuous circular motion until the vodka is thoroughly chilled (taking care not to chip the ice and dilute the vodka). Strain into a frosted martini glass and garnish with either a pitted olive or a lemon zest.

The Vodkatini has all but overtaken the original gin martini in popularity. As with the gin martini, there are four important things to consider when it comes to making a Vodkatini: the quantity of vermouth, to shake or stir, straight up or on the rocks and lastly, an olive or a twist. My preference is for the smallest hint of vermouth, stirred and served straight up with an olive.

vodkatini

sake
martini

The Sake Martini uses the heady combination of gin, vodka and sake, which might not sound very tempting, but take it from me, it's definitely worth having a try next time you order that takeaway sushi!

25 ml sake
25 ml vodka
a dash of gin

Pour the sake, vodka and a dash of gin into a mixing glass filled with ice. Stir the mixture until thoroughly chilled and strain into a frosted martini glass. Garnish with a slice of cucumber.

This pretty much says it all for the versatility of vodka and the extremes to which bartenders will go to create something new and off the wall. It's not a drink that I would recommend to accompany your cornflakes, unless first thing in the morning is actually last thing at night for you. If you fancy something a little more tangy, try replacing the orange marmalade with lime marmalade.

50 ml vodka
2 barspoons marmalade

Pour a large shot of vodka into a shaker filled with ice, add the marmalade, shake sharply and strain into a frosted martini glass.

breakfast martini

Kummel is one of the least frequently used liqueurs in cocktails, more's the pity. It has a distinctive, almost aniseed-like taste that comes from the caraway seeds used in its production, and as an added bonus it promotes good digestion. For the best results keep both the vodka and the kummel in a fridge or freezer and pour them gently into a sturdy old fashioned glass for the perfect after-dinner night cap.

silver
streak

25 ml chilled vodka
25 ml kummel

Pour a generous single measure of chilled vodka into a rocks glass filled with ice. Add a similar amount of kummel, stir gently and serve.

The upside of taking three or four minutes to create a drink that will only see the light of day for the same amount of time is the pleasure it gives the drinker. These days, shots have to be smooth, beguiling and potent, and they have to look good too. The Purple Haze is a classic Kamikaze with a twist – a drink that belies its strength and will kick-start any evening's fun. In the Detox, the combination of vodka, cranberry juice and peach schnapps is one that has been toyed with before but layering the ingredients allows the luxury of tasting them one at a time.

purple haze

25 ml vodka
1 white sugar cube
1 fresh lime
a dash of Grand Marnier
25 ml Chambord

Put a sugar cube and half a fresh lime, cut into quarters, into a shaker and crush them together with a muddler or barspoon. Add a single shot of vodka and a dash of Grand Marnier. Fill the shaker with ice, then shake and strain the mixture into a chilled shot glass. Float a single measure of Chambord onto the drink and serve.

25 ml peach schnapps
25 ml cranberry juice
25 ml vodka

Pour a small measure of ice-cold peach schnapps into a frosted shot glass; over the back of a barspoon, carefully layer an equal measure of cranberry juice so that it sits on top of the schnapps. Over the top of the cranberry juice layer a similar amount of ice-cold vodka. Serve.

detox

moscow
mule

50 ml vodka
1 lime
ginger beer

Pour a large measure of vodka
into a highball filled with ice.
Squeeze a lime, cut into
quarters, into the glass. Top with
ginger beer and stir with a
barspoon. Serve with a straw.

brazilian
mule

25 ml vodka
12.5 ml peppermint schnapps
12.5 ml Stones Ginger Wine
1 measure of espresso coffee
a dash of sugar syrup
ginger beer

Add the vodka, peppermint
schnapps and ginger wine to
an ice-filled shaker. Pour in one
shot of espresso coffee and
sugar syrup to taste. Shake and
strain into a highball glass filled
with ice and top with ginger
beer. Garnish with coffee beans.

strawberry
mule

50 ml vodka
12.5 ml frais de bois
a dash of sugar syrup
3 fresh strawberries
fresh ginger
ginger beer

Muddle together two thin slices
of ginger and the strawberries
in a mixing glass. Add a large
shot of vodka, the frais de bois
and sugar syrup and shake and
strain through a sieve into a
highball glass filled with ice. Top
with ginger beer, stir and serve
with a strawberry.

mule

The creation of the Moscow Mule woke us up to the godsend that
is ginger beer. It lends the Mule its legendary kick and an easy
spiciness. These attributes, together with the versatility of vodka, led
to the creation of alternatives that, while being completely different
in taste, still use the basic Mule ingredients. Ginger beer can also be
mixed to great effect with dark rum or bourbon. In these recipes the
vodka can be substituted with either of these two – try for yourself.
The Strawberry Mule is perfect for an afternoon in the sun, while
the Brazilian Mule is great after dinner.

The Vodka Espresso is a drink that not only portrays the flexibility of the spirit quite magnificently, but also brings to the cocktail world a drink with a combination punch. The drink originated (and, as with all cocktail stories, this should be taken with a pinch of salt) in a New York bar with a supermodel, who shall remain nameless, asking a bartender for something different to give her a zing. The concoction that the bartender presented her with was a little special. With a dark velvety body and creamy top, it was designed both to wake her up and to calm her down simultaneously.

50 ml vodka
1 measure espresso coffee
a dash of sugar syrup

Pour the espresso coffee into a shaker, add a large measure of vodka and sugar syrup to taste, shake the mixture up sharply and strain into an old fashioned glass filled with ice. Garnish with three coffee beans.

vodka
espresso

double
vision

This clean, elegant drink tastes too good to have any negative side effects but don't be fooled! The combination of Absolut Citron and Kurrant, plus the crisp apple juice, lends a deceptively light, summer feel to the cocktail.

25 ml Absolut Citron Vodka
25 ml Absolut Kurrant Vodka
2 dashes Angostura bitters
fresh apple juice

Pour single measures of both Absolut Citron and Kurrant into a glass filled with ice. Fill with fresh apple juice and add a couple of dashes of Angostura bitters. Stir with a barspoon and garnish with a squeezed lime quarter. Serve with a straw.

Strictly speaking, a sour, as its name suggests, should err on the tart side. However, as cocktails become more subjective and bartenders more accommodating, sours are taking on a slightly less sharp taste for those with a sweeter tooth. Thus came the Krupnik Sour – really not very sour at all because of the sweet vodka base, but altogether a most pleasant drinking experience.

krupnik
sour

50 ml Krupnik Vodka
50 ml fresh lemon juice
25 ml sugar syrup
25 ml egg white
2 dashes of Angostura bitters

Add all the ingredients to a shaker filled with ice. Shake the mixture and pour into an old fashioned glass. Garnish with a lemon slice and a maraschino cherry.

50 ml vodka
12.5 ml Galliano
fresh orange juice

Pour a large measure of vodka into a highball glass filled with ice. Fill the glass almost to the top with orange juice and pour in a float of Galliano. Garnish with an orange slice and serve with a swizzle stick and a straw.

harvey wallbanger

The story goes that Harvey, a Californian surfer who had performed particularly badly in an important contest, visited his local bar to drown his sorrows. He ordered his usual screwdriver – only to decide that it wasn't strong enough for what he had in mind. Scanning the bar for something to boost his drink, his eyes fell on the distinctively shaped Galliano bottle, a shot of which was then added to his drink as a float. Needless to say, his resultant state after a few of these was so rocky that, as he searched for the door on the way home, he bounced off a couple of walls before spilling out onto the street. Harvey Wallbanger they called him.

Modern, thirst-quenching variations on the classic screwdriver completely mask the taste of the vodka, so they are very popular with people who don't really enjoy the taste of alcohol. The cranberry juice lends a light, fruity, refreshing quality to these cocktails – slightly bitter in the Sea Breeze but softened in the Madras by the orange juice. The Tropical Breeze followed, using flavoured vodka. Any combination of vodka and freshly squeezed juices will work in creating a Breeze to suit your personal taste.

50 ml vodka
cranberry juice
fresh grapefruit juice

Pour a large shot of vodka into a highball filled with ice. Three quarters fill the glass with cranberry juice and top with fresh grapefruit juice. Garnish with a lime quarter and serve with a straw.

sea
breeze

tropical
breeze

50 ml Wyborowa Melon Vodka
cranberry juice
fresh grapefruit juice

Pour a large measure of melon-
flavoured vodka into a highball
glass filled with ice. Top with
equal amounts of cranberry and
fresh grapefruit juice. Garnish
with a melon ball.

50 ml vodka
cranberry juice
fresh orange juice

Pour a large measure of vodka
into a highball glass filled with
ice. Top with equal amounts of
cranberry juice and orange juice
and garnish with an orange
slice. Serve with a straw.

madras

The Black and White Russian are classics that have been on the scene for many a year. They make stylish after-dinner cocktails with their sweet coffee flavour, which is sharpened up by the vodka. The White Russian, with its addition of the cream float, is even more appropriate as a nightcap.

black
russian

50 ml vodka
25 ml kahlúa coffee liqueur

Shake the vodka and kahlúa together over ice and strain into a rocks glass filled with ice.

white
russian

For a White Russian, layer 25 ml single cream into the glass of Black Russian over the back of a barspoon. For both variations, garnish with a stemmed cherry.

gin

Gin has been the base for a great many of the world's most revered cocktails and has sat contentedly on the shelves of some of the swankiest cocktail bars of all time.

However, it was not always the case. At the beginning of the 18th century gin was the poor man's tipple – a coarse, sweetened spirit, unlike the very much more refined dry gin of today.

Gin became popular in cocktails during the Prohibition in the United States. Easier and cheaper to make in a bathtub than whisky but still very poor in quality, mixers were added to the drink to improve the taste. Despite gin's rather dubious beginnings, Americans developed a taste for the spirit, particularly in the form of the Dry Martini, and whose popularity was almost certainly helped by the number of celebrity drinkers of this most chic of all cocktails, including such luminaries as Ernest Hemingway, Winston Churchill, F D Roosevelt and W C Fields.

FDR martini

(ALSO KNOWN AS THE DIRTY MARTINI)
50 ml gin
a dash of dry vermouth
12.5 ml olive brine
1 green olive

Add the gin, a dash of dry vermouth
and the olive brine to a shaker filled
with cracked ice. Shake sharply and
strain into a frosted martini glass with a
lemon-zested rim. Garnish with an olive.

50 ml gin
a dash of dry vermouth
a dash of whisky

This is a variation on the FDR
Martini, with the whisky
substituting for the olive brine,
but the method is identical.

smoky martini

Winston Churchill, like many of his contemporaries, would search for ways to prevent his beloved martini being sabotaged by the inclusion of too much vermouth. So, whereas some just aromatize their martini with vermouth and others marinade their olives in vermouth, Churchill would merely look at the bottle when fixing himself a martini. Franklin D Roosevelt, who wasn't quite such a purist, carried a martini kit on international summits. One of his specialities, which he mixed for Joseph Stalin during a conference, was probably the first FDR Martini.

(ALSO KNOWN AS THE NAKED MARTINI)
50 ml gin
1 bottle dry vermouth

Using a mixing glass, chill a large shot of gin over ice and pour into a frosted martini glass. (An easier method is to keep a bottle of gin in the freezer.) Pass a bottle of vermouth over the drink, ensuring that the sun shines through the liquid onto the martini. Garnish with a green olive.

churchill
martini

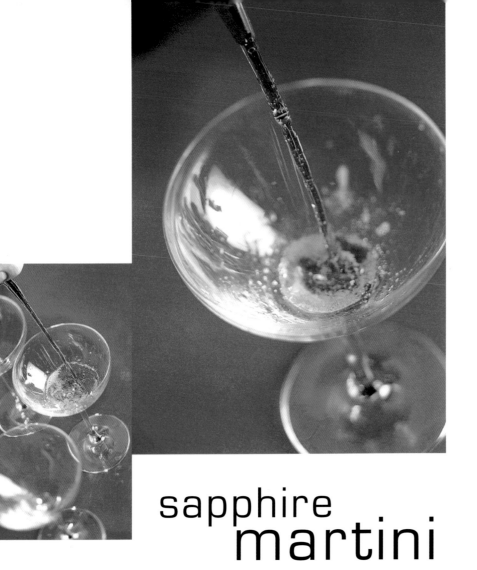

sapphire
martini

In an attempt to utilize one of those rarely used liqueurs often found nestled snugly at the back of the bar between the blue curaçao and the Galliano, I stumbled across an amazingly simple variation on the martini. Bombay Sapphire gin, with its spicy notes, was the perfect match for the Parfait d'Amour. Although unpromising on its own, being sickly sweet and tasting slightly of flower petals and lavender, a couple of drops of the very blue Parfait d'Amour combined with well-chilled Bombay Sapphire Gin produces a magnificent cocktail. It's not to everyone's taste, granted, but it's a subtle martini variation that can sit proudly on any cocktail menu.

50 ml Bombay Sapphire Gin
a dash of Parfait d'Amour

Gently pour the Parfait
d'Amour into a frosted
martini glass. Over a
barspoon, pour the gin
(which should have been
in the freezer for at least
1 hour) so that it sits over
the blue liqueur. Garnish
with blueberries on a
cocktail stick.

Two offshoots of the original Gin Fizz, a classic that some would say should remain untouched. However, these cocktails have now become fashionable in their own right. The substitution of the soda by champagne in the Royal Gin Fizz helps to make this cocktail special and lends it a little extra fizz (surely no harm there!), whilst the addition of the rose flower water in the New Orleans or Ramos Gin Fizz accentuates the juniper flavour in the gin and the dash of cream gives this very light drink a little more body.

royal gin fizz

50 ml gin
25 ml fresh lemon juice
1 barspoon white sugar (or
   12.5 ml sugar syrup)
champagne
1 egg white

Put the egg white, gin, lemon juice and sugar into a shaker filled with ice and shake vigorously. Strain into a collins glass filled with ice. Top with champagne and garnish with a slice of lemon.

new orleans fizz

(ALSO KNOWN AS THE RAMOS GIN FIZZ)
50 ml gin
25 ml fresh lemon juice
1 barspoon white sugar (or
   12.5 ml sugar syrup)
12.5 ml rose flower water (or
   orange flower water)
12.5 ml single cream
a dash of egg white
soda water

Add all the ingredients, except the soda water, to a shaker filled with ice. Shake vigorously and strain into a highball over ice. Gently add the soda water, stirring with a barspoon while doing so, and garnish with a lemon slice.

part of **the pleasure** of drinking a cocktail is admiring its **good looks**

This drink has, like many others before it, evolved from the recipe for another successful cocktail. Using the basic sling recipe that appears in such classics as the Singapore Sling, we replace the cherry brandy float with crème de mure (made from blackberries) and Hey Presto! a new cocktail (it's not as hard as it may seem).

Part of the pleasure of drinking a cocktail is admiring its good looks, and with this recipe, the drink would taste exactly the same if the mure was added to the shaker with the other ingredients, rather than adding it at the end, but it certainly would not look as glamorous.

With the sharpness of the gin and the sweetness of the mure melting the crushed ice – but not quite merging – this is the perfect long cocktail for drinking on a sunny deck or verandah in the cool of an early evening.

50 ml gin
25 ml fresh lime juice
12.5 ml sugar syrup
25 ml crème de mure

Add the gin, lime juice and
sugar syrup to a shaker filled
with ice. Shake the mixture and
strain into a sling glass. Fill with
crushed ice and pour in the
crème de mure gently so that
the liquid sinks to the bottom of
the cocktail. Garnish with a slice
of lemon and a fresh blackberry.

gin
bramble

pink gin

50 ml gin
a dash of Angostura bitters

Rinse a frosted sherry or martini glass with Angostura bitters, add chilled gin and serve.

Pink Gin is a thoroughly English cocktail which, although it originated as a medicinal potion in the British navy, became one of the smartest drinks in 1940s' London. Like the Gimlet it deserves a premium gin. The Gimlet is among those drinks that can easily be ruined if the flavour of the gin is drowned by an over-generous measure of cordial. It should be shaken vigorously to ensure that the cocktail is chilled to perfection then strained carefully before serving to catch any chips of ice.

gin
gimlet

50 ml gin
25 ml lime cordial

Pour the gin and cordial into a
shaker filled with ice. Shake very
sharply and strain through a sieve
into a frosted martini glass.

a New York speciality from the jazz age

The Bronx dates back to the days of Prohibition, when gang bosses reigned and booze played an important part in the economy of the underworld. Different areas of New York became known for the special cocktails they offered, such as this speciality of the Bronx district. Like the Manhattan, it has three variations: the dry, the sweet and the perfect. The Silver and Golden Bronx are variations on the perfect with the addition of egg white or egg yolk.

silver bronx

50 ml gin
a dash of dry vermouth
a dash of sweet vermouth
50 ml fresh orange juice
1 egg white

Shake all the ingredients vigorously over ice and strain into a chilled cocktail glass.

golden bronx

The method is the same as above, but substitute the egg white for an egg yolk.

25 ml gin
a dash of sweet vermouth
a dash of dry vermouth
2 dashes of fresh lemon juice
2 dashes of triple sec
2 dashes of Angostura bitters

Shake all the ingredients over ice and strain into a frosted martini glass.

the
journalist

I've never been a supporter of unnecessarily complicated cocktails but this one seems to succeed against all the odds. The Journalist defies convention but is great as a palate-cleansing aperitif. The sweet/dry theme is repeated twice, with the sweet and dry vermouth, then the triple sec and lemon juice. Definitely a good pre-dinner drink to order at a bar, but if you are making it at home watch the measurements carefully; it's a drink that needs to be very finely balanced.

whisky

Of all the spirits, whisky is the least frequently used in cocktails, although it brings to the table as much variety (if not more) as the next spirit. Whisky lovers might cringe at the thought of anything more flavoursome than water being added to their sacred drink but in fact it does make the perfect base for some of the best-known cocktails. In fairness, many of the whisky-based cocktails originated in the United States and so traditionally would contain bourbon or rye whiskey, which were not treated with quite such reverence as Scottish whisky.

Made predominately in four countries, all whiskies are grain-based (although using a variety of grains) but are subjected to different methods of preparation, distillation and ageing. For quick reference, Scottish and Canadian whiskies are spelt without the 'e' and US and Irish with.

Because of the huge range of flavours in whiskies, the choice of which to use in a cocktail will be somewhat subjective. Many may swear by Canadian Club in their Dry Manhattan but will go for the smoother, more rounded taste of Maker's Mark bourbon in their Perfect Manhattan. Ranging from the medicinal uses of the Hot Toddy – a great drink and excuse for one – to the refreshing effect of a Mint Julep, whisky in cocktails can play the roles of both comforter and revitalizer. My advice is don't wait until you think you are the right age to drink whisky before trying it in a cocktail.

manhattan

The naming of Manhattan Island has an anecdotal history that links it with the Manhattan cocktail. At the start of the 17th century, Henry Hudson served a dark spirit to the Lenape Indians on an unnamed island. The Indians became rather drunk and, on recovering, named the island 'Manhachtanienck', roughly translated as 'the island where we became intoxicated', a name which evolved into Manhattan. Whether or not the story has any historical value, it's a great thought that Manhattan the island gained its name from an experience with the Manhattan cocktail's main ingredient (definitely my sort of town!).

perfect
manhattan

50 ml rye whiskey
12.5 ml sweet vermouth
12.5 ml dry vermouth
a dash of Angostura bitters
1 lemon zest garnish

dry
manhattan

50 ml rye whiskey
25 ml dry vermouth
a dash of Angostura bitters
1 maraschino cherry garnish

sweet
manhattan

50 ml rye whiskey
25 ml sweet vermouth
a dash of orange bitters
1 orange zest garnish

For each of the variations, add the
ingredients to a mixing glass filled
with ice (ensure all ingredients are
very cold) and stir the mixture until
chilled. Strain into a frosted martini
glass, add the garnish and serve.

rusty nail

30 ml whisky
30 ml Drambuie

Add both ingredients to a glass filled with ice and muddle with a barspoon. Garnish with a zest of orange.

boston sour

50 ml bourbon
25 ml fresh lemon juice
2 barspoons sugar syrup
2 dashes of Angostura bitters
a dash of egg white

Add all the ingredients to a shaker filled with ice and shake sharply. Strain the contents into a whisky tumbler filled with ice, garnish with a lemon slice and a maraschino cherry.

The classic Old Fashioned is a drink that demands attention from its maker. Despite the relative simplicity of its ingredients, neglect the detail of the preparation at your peril. The delicate mix of sugar and orange zest will bring to life whichever bourbon you choose to use. The Rusty Nail is quick to mix but always delights with its simple combination of Scotch whisky and honey liqueur – perfect to drink by a log fire on a chilly evening. The classic sour is made with Scotch, but since I like my sours a little on the sweet side I prefer the vanillary sweetness of this bourbon-based sour.

50 ml bourbon
1 white sugar cube
2 dashes of orange bitters
a strip of orange zest

Place the sugar cube soaked with orange bitters into a rocks glass, muddle the mixture with a barspoon and add a dash of bourbon and a couple of ice cubes. Keep adding ice and bourbon and keep muddling until the full 50 ml has been added to the glass (ensuring the sugar has dissolved). Rim the glass with a zest of orange and drop it into the glass.

old fashioned

hot toddy

50 ml whisky
25 ml fresh lemon juice
2 barspoons honey or sugar syrup
75 ml hot water
1 cinnamon stick
5 whole cloves
2 lemon slices

Skewer the cloves into the lemon slices and add them to a heatproof glass or a toddy glass along with the rest of the ingredients.

The Hot Toddy, with its warming blend of spices and sweet honey aroma, is the perfect comforter and will soothe any aches, snuffles and alcohol withdrawal symptoms that your illness may have inflicted upon you. It's also a great life-saver for cold afternoons spent outside watching sport. Next time you have need to pack a thermos flask of coffee, think again – mix up a batch of Hot Toddies, and see how much more popular you are than the next man!

50 ml bourbon
2 sugar cubes
5 sprigs of mint

Crush the mint and sugar cubes
in the bottom of a collins glass.
Fill the glass with crushed ice
and add the bourbon. Stir
the mixture vigorously with
a barspoon and serve.

mint julep

Two serious cocktails here. The Mint Julep, as the base spirit suggests, originated in the
American deep south, although the term 'julep' derives from the Arabic word *julab*,
meaning rose water. Try substituting white or dark rum or brandy for the bourbon, or, if
you really feel you deserve a treat, add champagne to the mint and sugar for one of the
more refreshing tipples on the cocktail menu. The Sazarac can be topped with water
or soda to make a thirst quencher but to fully enjoy the flavours it should be drunk
undiluted. If, like me, you enjoy the lingering flavour of pastis, try adding the Pernod
to the drink rather than rinsing the glass with it.

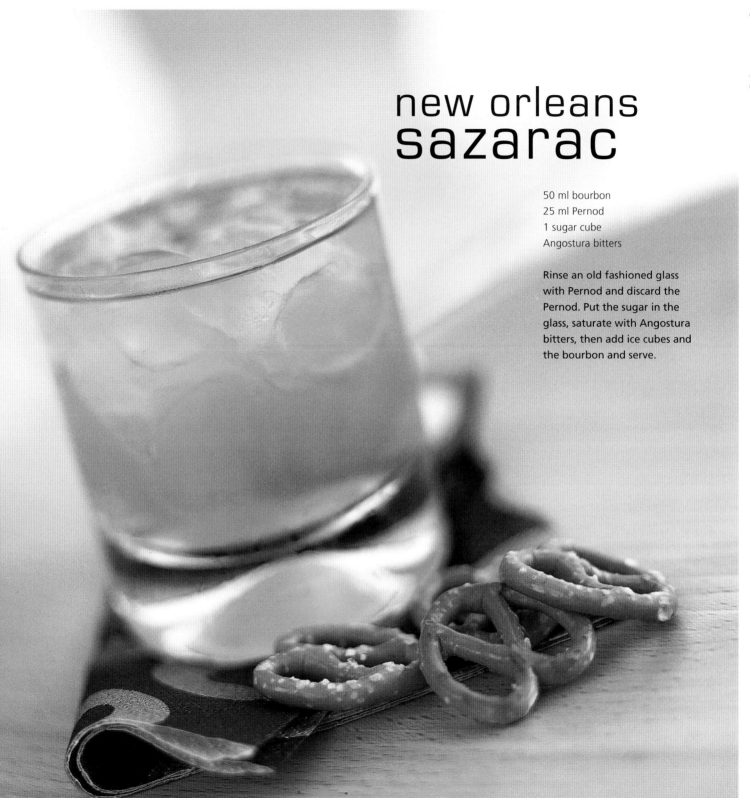

new orleans
sazarac

50 ml bourbon
25 ml Pernod
1 sugar cube
Angostura bitters

Rinse an old fashioned glass
with Pernod and discard the
Pernod. Put the sugar in the
glass, saturate with Angostura
bitters, then add ice cubes and
the bourbon and serve.

blue blazer

50 ml whisky
50 ml boiling water
1 sugar cube

Warm two small metal tankards. In one, dissolve the sugar in the boiling water. In the other pour the whisky. Set the whisky alight, and as it burns, pour the liquid into the first tumbler and back, from one to another, creating a continuous stream of fire. Once the flame has died down, pour the mixture into a warmed old fashioned glass and garnish with a sprinkle of nutmeg.

A spectacular drink to serve but one that is best practised in the safe confines of the kitchen before trying it in front of an audience. Another tip for those of you who are itching to light up your favourite pewter tankards: unless they have heat-resistant handles, burnt fingers may be the result of your first attempt at this cocktail! In order to keep the whisky burning, it helps if the tankards have been warmed first. When pouring the liquid back and forth, keep the tankards relatively close together until you've got a rhythm going. There are a number of cocktails that can be created using a naked flame but these drinks are best kept for the start of the evening, for obvious reasons. By and large, the use of a flame in cocktail preparation is for show but since part of the bartender's job is to entertain then if that means a couple of lightly singed eyebrows then so be it!

rum

WORLD'S OLDEST RUM
SINCE 1703

Gold

Cocktail bartenders spend a great deal of time and effort getting creative, searching for the ultimate magic formula that will continue the recent popularity of cocktails.

Personally, I believe that rum (widely tipped as the new vodka, a theory I subscribe to wholeheartedly) is the spirit that will lead cocktails forward.

Diverse in taste and strength, rum is distilled from sugar cane and made wherever the crop is grown, although the Caribbean leads in production. From those islands we have Jamaican rums (dark golden), Barbadian and Trinidadian (light and dry), Guyanan (dark and heavy), and perhaps the best known, Bacardi from Cuba – a white or golden rum.

Considering the provenance of rum, it's not surprising that a great many rum cocktails are mixed with fresh juices, especially lime. A great classic of today, the Daiquiri (rum, lime juice and sugar syrup), is just one of these very successful combinations.

orange
daiquiri

50 ml Creole Schrubb Rum
12.5 ml fresh lemon juice
1 barspoon sugar syrup

Measure all the ingredients and
pour into an ice-filled shaker.
Shake and strain through a sieve
into a frosted martini glass.

The Daiquiri is a classic cocktail that was made
famous at the El Floridita restaurant, Havana,
early in the 20th century. It has as many recipe
variations as famous drinkers (Hemingway
always ordered doubles at El Floridita) but
once you have found the perfect balance of
light (traditionally Cuban) rum, sharp citrus
juice and sweet sugar syrup then stick to those
measurements exactly. The Orange Daiquiri
substitutes the sweet Martinique rum for the
Cuban so use a little less sugar syrup to keep
that delicate balance of sharp and sweet.

original daiquiri

50 ml golden rum
12.5 ml fresh lime juice
2 barspoons sugar syrup

Measure all the ingredients and pour
into an ice-filled shaker. Shake and
strain into a frosted martini glass.

These cocktails are two perfect examples of rum's affinity with fresh juices. Rum also has the ability to hold its own when combined with quite a selection of other flavours. The Rum Punch, for instance, traditionally mixed in a large bowl, often with a random selection of ingredients thrown in, still tastes predominantly of rum (assuming a good measure of rum is used!).

jamaican breeze

50 ml white rum
2 slices fresh ginger
75 ml cranberry juice
75 ml fresh pineapple juice

Pound the ginger and rum together in the bottom of a shaker with a barspoon or muddler, then add ice and the remaining ingredients. Shake and strain into a highball glass filled with ice.

25 ml white rum
25 ml dark rum
juice of 1 lime
a dash of sugar syrup
150 ml fresh pineapple juice

Shake all the ingredients sharply
over ice in a shaker and strain
into a highball glass filled with
crushed ice.

rum
runner

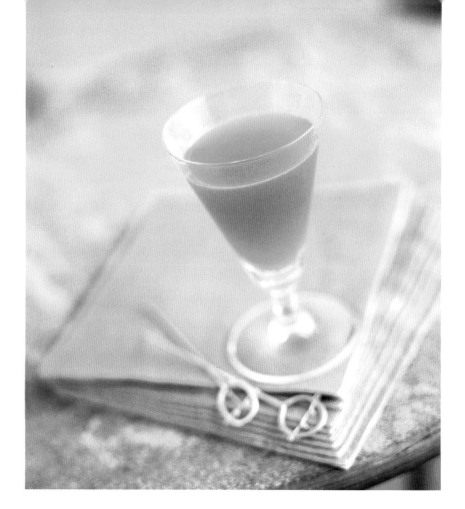

bacardi
cocktail

50 ml Bacardi white rum
a dash of grenadine
juice of 1 small lime
1 barspoon of powdered sugar or
   a dash of sugar syrup

Shake all the ingredients sharply
over ice, then strain into a frosted
martini glass and serve.

One of the best-known Daiquiri variations and one
that must be made with the Bacardi brand of white
rum, as decreed by a New York court action in 1936.

For those who love the idea of a martini but refuse to be budged from drinking rum-based cocktails (an honourable but distinctly narrow-minded point of view) the Black Dog is the answer.

50 ml light rum
a dash of dry vermouth
1 black olive

Add the rum and vermouth to a mixing glass filled with ice and stir rhythmically and gently. Once the mixture is thoroughly chilled, strain into a frosted martini glass and garnish with a black olive.

black dog

50 ml golden rum
25 ml coconut cream
12.5 ml cream
25 ml fresh pineapple juice

Put all the ingredients into a blender, add an ice scoop of crushed ice and blend. Pour into a sour or collins glass and garnish with a thick slice of pineapple.

honey colada

For a Honey Colada, add 2 barspoons of honey or sugar syrup to the glass after the drink has been poured:

piña colada

A sweet, creamy drink that, for a time, epitomized the the kind of cocktail that 'real' cocktail drinkers disapproved of (compare a Piña Colada with a Dry Martini!). However, since its creation in the 1970s, it has won widespread popularity, and now that we are in the new millennium, cocktails are for everyone so there's no shame in ordering a Piña Colada at the bar. Try the Honey Colada variation for a sweet surprise lurking at the bottom of the glass (only for the very sweet-toothed). Alternatively, use the Mexican liqueur kahlú as the base, for a light coffee taste.

50 ml Demerara rum
12.5 ml orange curaçao
12.5 ml apricot brandy
12.5 ml fresh lemon or lime juice
a dash of Angostura bitters
2 dashes of orgeat syrup
12.5 ml fresh pineapple juice
a mint sprig

Add all the ingredients to a
cocktail shaker filled with ice,
shake and strain into a ice-filled
old fashioned glass. Garnish
with a pineapple slice and a
mint sprig. Serve with straws.

mai tai

With a complex mixture of flavours, this cocktail has as many variations as
it has garnishes. This drink is always a good litmus test for a new bar; find
somewhere that makes a good Mai Tai and you can be sure they'll be good
for most others cocktails. For a good example of how a Mai Tai should taste,
try the one at Trader Vic's, next to the Met Bar in London – definitely one of
my favourites. The one thing that most bartenders seem to agree on is that a
thick, dark rum should be used along with all the fruit-based ingredients that
lend the classic its legendary fruitiness.

The Planter's Punch recipe can never be forgotton since Myers have very kindly put the recipe on the back label of their rum bottle. A great favourite for parties because it can be made in advance. It could be prepared in an old oak barrel for authenticity but a big bowl will do, with slices of fruit added, such as oranges, melons, apples and pears. Try to make it at least a couple of hours before the party so that the flavours can meld together, then add the soda and ice at the last minute. The T-Punch is a refreshing drink, perfect for a hot summer day, which can be made according to taste with more lime or more sugar for quick variation.

planter's punch

50 ml Myers rum
juice of half a lemon
50 ml fresh orange juice
a dash of sugar syrup
soda water

Pour all the ingredients, except the soda water, into a cocktail shaker filled with ice, shake and strain into a ice-filled highball. Top up with soda water and garnish with a slice of orange.

t-punch

50 ml white rum
1 lime
1 brown sugar cube
soda water

Place the sugar cube in the bottom of an old fashioned glass. Cut the lime into eighths, squeeze and drop into the glass. Pound with a pestle to break up the sugar. Add the rum and ice, then top up with soda water. Stir and serve.

mojito

The Mojito emerged in London over the summer of '98 as the thinking man's refreshment tipple. With its alluring mix of mint and rum, it invariably whisked him away from whatever feeble attempt the English sun was making at shining and transported him to warmer, more tropical climes.

50 ml golden rum
5 sprigs of mint
2 dashes of sugar syrup
a dash of fresh lime juice
soda water

Put the mint into a highball, add the rum, lime juice and sugar syrup and pound with a barspoon until the aroma of the mint is released. Add the crushed ice and stir vigorously until the mixture and the mint is spread evenly. Top with soda water and stir again. Serve with straws.

cuba libre

One of the most famous of all rum-based drinks was reputed to have been invented by an army officer in Cuba shortly after Coca Cola was first produced in the 1890s.

50 ml white rum
1 lime
cola

Pour the rum into a highball filled with ice; cut a lime into eighths, squeeze and drop the wedges into the glass. Top with cola and serve with straws.

rum is the perfect base for some great summer cocktails, here combined with fresh, sharp limes

cachaça

Cachaça, a spirit indigenous to Brazil is distilled directly from the juice of sugar cane, unlike white rum, which is usually distilled from molasses. The Caipirinha has made cachaça popular in many countries.

caipirinha

50 ml cachaça
1 lime
2 brown sugar cubes

Cut the lime into eighths, squeeze and place into an old fashioned glass with the sugar cubes, then pound well with a pestle. Fill the glass with crushed ice and add the cachaça. Stir vigorously and serve with a straw.

azure martini

50 ml cachaça
12.5 ml canella liqueur
a dash of fresh lime or lemon juice
a dash of sugar syrup
½ apple

Pound the apple in the bottom of a cocktail shaker to release the flavour. Add crushed ice and the remaining ingredients, shake and strain through a sieve into a frosted martini glass.

passion fruit batida

25 ml cachaça
25 ml passion fruit juice
25 ml fresh pineapple juice
a dash of passion fruit syrup
a dash of lime syrup
a dash of fresh lime juice

Mix all the ingredients in a blender, strain into a small highball glass over crushed ice.

brandy

aperitifs & liqueurs

Brandy is a wonderful, warming spirit distilled from wine. The best-known is Cognac and Armagnac from France, but most other wine-producing countries also make excellent brandies. Long, slow ageing in oak barrels gives brandy a rich smoothness and the top-quality examples should undoubtedly be appreciated on their own. It is, though, a surprisingly versatile spirit that mixes well with many other flavours.

According to Samuel Johnson, brandy was once considered to be the drink for men who aspire to be heroes, but times have changed and now it is enjoyed by men and women alike.

Aperitifs, broadly speaking, are drinks that are taken before a meal to sharpen the appetite, but the term is also used to describe patent drinks that are made specifically for this purpose. I have included some cocktails that combine aperitifs, sometimes with other flavours, to great effect.

Liqueurs, which are sweetened spirits flavoured with spices, herbs, flowers and so on, offer great possibilities when making cocktails, adding magical colours and a balancing sweetness. Liqueurs are used throughout this book alongside other spirits but in this section they appear on their own, centre stage.

50 ml brandy
25 ml crème de menthe (white)

Shake the ingredients together over ice and strain into a frosted martini glass.

stinger

The Stinger is a great palate cleanser and digestif and like brandy should be consumed after dinner. The amount of crème de menthe added depends on personal taste: too much and the result is akin to liquid toothpaste, another palate cleanser, but not with the same effects unfortunately. The Sidecar, like many of the classic cocktails created in the 1920s, is attributed to the inventive genius of Harry MacElhone, who founded Harry's New York Bar in Paris. It is said to have been created in honour of an eccentric military man who would roll up outside the bar in the sidecar of his chauffeur-driven motorcycle. It is certainly the cocktail choice of people who know precisely what they want.

50 ml brandy
juice of half a lemon
12.5 ml Cointreau

Shake all the ingredients
together over ice and strain
into a frosted martini glass
with a sugared rim.

sidecar

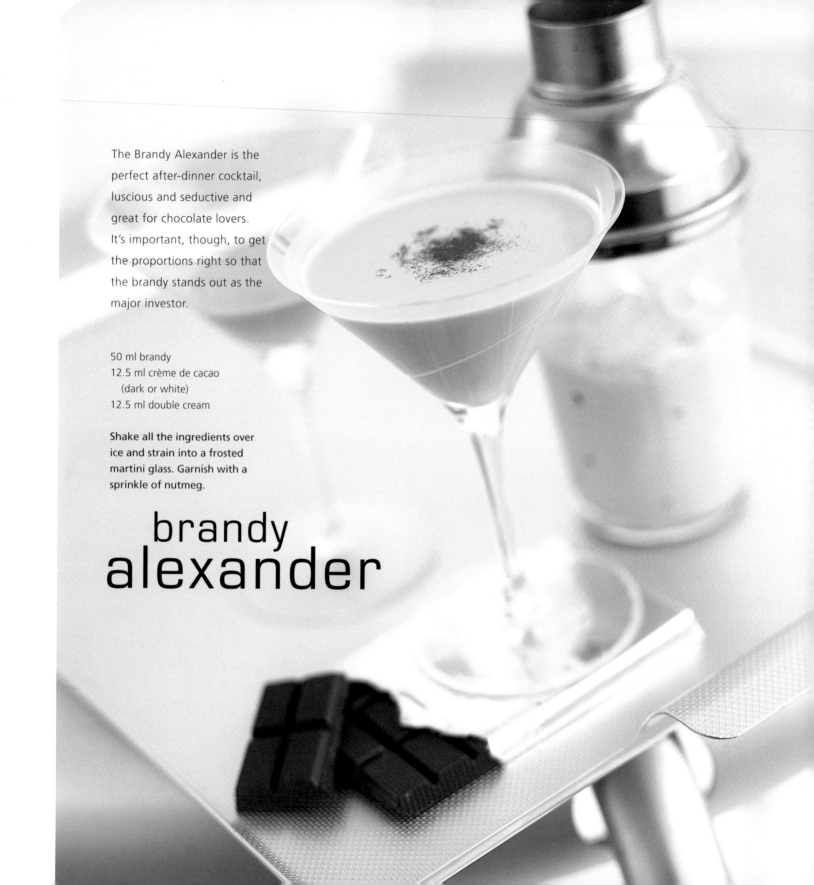

The Brandy Alexander is the perfect after-dinner cocktail, luscious and seductive and great for chocolate lovers. It's important, though, to get the proportions right so that the brandy stands out as the major investor.

50 ml brandy
12.5 ml crème de cacao
    (dark or white)
12.5 ml double cream

Shake all the ingredients over ice and strain into a frosted martini glass. Garnish with a sprinkle of nutmeg.

brandy
alexander

cynar
cocktail

Cynar is an artichoke-based aperitif made in Italy. Bizarre though it may sound, it actually makes a creditable cocktail, particularly when mixed with its fellow Italian aperitif, vermouth.

25 ml Cynar
25 ml dry vermouth
an orange wedge

Pour the Cynar and vermouth into an aperitif glass filled with ice and stir. Squeeze a wedge of orange over the glass, drop it in and serve.

sour
italian

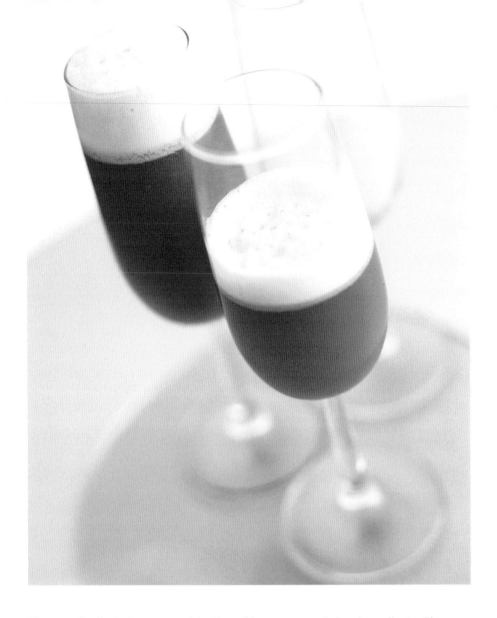

25 ml Campari
12.5 ml Strega
12.5 ml Galliano
25 ml fresh lemon juice
12.5 ml cranberry juice
12.5 ml sugar syrup
a dash of egg white
2 dashes of Angostura bitters

Shake all the ingredients over ice and strain into a wine glass.

americano

25 ml Campari
25 ml sweet vermouth
soda water
1 orange slice

Build the ingredients over ice into a highball glass, stir and serve with an orange slice.

Three cocktails that use a combination of home-grown Italian ingredients. The Negroni and the Americano have, of course, been around for a long time, but the Sour Italian was my attempt, whilst staying in Tuscany, to create a new, completely Italian cocktail. It made the ideal aperitif. The Americano is a refreshing blend of bitter and sweet, topped with soda to make the perfect thirst quencher for a hot summer afternoon. The Negroni packs a powerful punch but still makes an elegant aperitif. For a drier variation, add a little more dry gin, but if a fruitier cocktail is more to your taste, wipe some orange zest around the top of the glass and add some to the drink.

negroni

25 ml Campari
25 ml sweet vermouth
25 ml gin

Build all the ingredients into
a rocks glass filled with ice,
garnish with an orange zest and
stir. For an extra-dry Negroni,
add a little more gin.

the mystique
of absinthe is heightened by
its all-important ritual

50 ml absinthe
1 barspoon white sugar
50 ml still mineral water

absinthe
cocktail

Absinthe is enjoying a revival in London bars after some notoriety in the early 20th century put it out of favour (in fact in some countries it was and still is banned). The infusion of wormwood (*absinthe* in French) was believed to endanger health but any casualties were much more likely to have been the result of its high alcohol content. It's around 70 per cent proof – so it's probably best to stick to one! If you have difficulty obtaining absinthe, try making an Absinthe Suissesse, which uses Pernod instead, together with dashes of anisette, orange flower water, white crème de menthe and an egg white, shaken over ice and served in a cocktail glass.

Pour the absinthe into an old fashioned glass. Dip the barspoon of sugar into the liquid, ensuring the absinthe saturates the sugar. Set light to the sugar and hold it over the glass until the sugar begins to caramelize, then drop the mixture into the liquid. If the liquid begins to burn, keep stirring the mixture until the sugar has all but dissolved (taking care not to crack the glass). Add the mineral water to taste, stir one last time and serve.

grasshopper

25 ml crème de menthe (white)
12.5 ml crème de menthe (green)
25 ml single cream

Shake all the ingredients over
ice, strain into a frosted martini
glass and serve.

There seems to be no midway for cocktails that contain cream – people either love them or hate them. Personally, I think there is a time and a place for any drink and these two should definitely be reserved for after dinner. The Golden Cadillac is not a drink to be approached lightly, and you could be excused for raising your eyebrows at the possibility of mixing crème de cacao (chocolate flavoured) with orange juice and Galliano (herb and liquorice flavoured). If the thought of this combination is too much for you, try substituting the crème de cacao with Cointreau for another popular cocktail called Golden Dream. The Grasshopper is a more obvious combination of peppermint and cream, the perfect drink to accompany your after-dinner coffee.

golden
cadillac

25 ml crème de cacao (white)
25 ml single cream
50 ml fresh orange juice
a dash of Galliano

Shake all the ingredients over ice, strain into a martini glass and serve.

tequila

... ...g.owing popularity on both sides of the Atlantic as the fashionable good-time drink.

Made in Mexico from the distinctively flavoured agave plant, tequila has not only the character to stand up where other spirits lie down but also the strength to give you a little slap around the face as it hits the spot.

The distinctly ritualistic methods of imbibing tequila also have their origins in Mexico. From the tequila shot (with its lick, sip, suck, order of service) to the tequila slammer (with its macho methods of preparation and drinking), there is always much fun and face-pulling to be had when tequila is on the menu.

Tequila Bianco and Reposado mix well with other spirits and mixers and tequilas with the appellation Añejo, which have been kept for at least a year, are best reserved for sipping with a chilled glass of spiced tomato juice on the side.

50 ml gold tequila
25 ml triple sec (or Cointreau)
Juice of half a lime

Shake all the ingredients sharply
with cracked ice. Strain into a
chilled cocktail glass rimmed
with salt.

margarita

Cut the lime into eighths, squeeze and place in an old fashioned glass with sugar syrup, then pound well with a pestle. Fill the glass with ice and add the tequila. Stir and serve.

conmemorativo

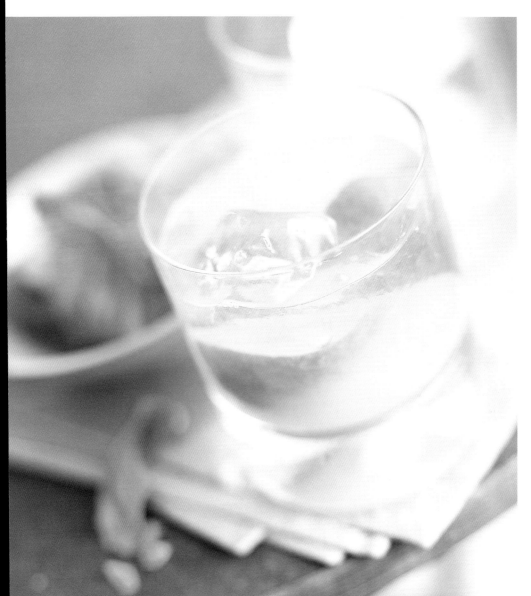

The Margarita is the cocktail most closely associated with tequila. This is the classic recipe, but when you are making it at home there is no right or wrong way – just your way! You can use Cointreau or triple sec, lime or lemon juice or even cordial, but never, ever use a ready-made premix. The Conmemorativo is a variation on the Margarita that uses a premium, aged tequila. It was a New York band, the Fun Lovin' Criminals, who, during a night at the Met Bar in London, suggested that this special tequila could be used in a cocktail just so long as it was shown respect. Hence the Conmemorativo which, with its glass full of lime wedges, can only be sipped to be fully appreciated.

[tequila]

103

rude
cosmopolitan

50 ml gold tequila
12.5 ml triple sec
50 ml cranberry juice
juice of half a lime

**Shake all ingredients well over ice
and strain into a frosted martini
glass. Squeeze a strip of orange
zest, skin downwards over a flame
held over the glass. Serve.**

The Rude Cosmopolitan is so named because of the lengths you will go to,
empty glass in hand, to jump the queue at the bar. The first sensation when
drinking this cocktail is the aroma of caramelized orange (well worth the effort
of burning the zest), followed by the sharp tang of the lime juice combined
with the clarity of the cranberry juice, and finally, the oily taste of the tequila
that will remain in your mouth for as long as it takes to order another.

In complete contrast, the Tequila Slammer is the ultimate machismo drink
and one that needs to be handled with care. This one is more likely to be
imbibed for the sensation rather than the taste!

50 ml gold tequila
50 ml champagne (chilled)

Pour both the tequila and the
chilled champagne into a small
collins glass with a sturdy base.
Hold a napkin over the glass
(sealing the liquid inside).
Sharply slam the glass down on
a stable surface and drink in one
go as the drink is fizzing.

tequila slammer

with the tomato juice, which is chilled and flavoured with lemon juice. The gold tequila combines very effectively with the tomato juice, its oily aftertaste making it more of a stalker than a chaser! This cocktail doesn't disguise the taste of any of its components – it just emphasizes their great working relationship.

50 ml gold tequila
50 ml tomato juice (chilled)
a dash of fresh lemon juice
a sprinkle of freshly ground
    black pepper

Pour the tequila (unchilled) into a shot glass. Add the tomato juice to another shot glass and mix in the lemon juice and pepper. These drinks should be sipped alternately.

the sangrita

champagne

...pagne is well chilled and on its own. However, when champagne is mixed with ingredients that enhance its taste, the results can be dramatic. The finest and best-known champagne cocktails tend to marry the champagne with just one other drink (brandy, orange juice, Guinness) to produce a stunning combination of looks and flavours.

If, however, champagne is deemed too great an extravagance to mix with other drinks, there is always the cheaper alternative of using sparkling wine. The rules for mixing champagne cocktails are very simple: always keep the champagne well chilled; always add the champagne last to the cocktail to keep the fizz; and finally, (and rather obviously!) never add champagne to a shaker.

champagne cocktails are perfect for inducing the party spirit

belli

The Bellini orig:
Harry's Bar in V
early 1940s and
favourite of the movers and
shakers of chic society.
Although there are many
variations on this recipe,
there is one golden rule for
the perfect Bellini – always
use fresh, ripe peaches to
make the peach juice.

¼ fresh peach, skinned
12.5 ml crème de peche
a dash of peach bitters (optional)
champagne

**Blend the peach and add to a
champagne flute. Pour in the
crème de peche and the peach
bitters, if using, and gently top
up with champagne, stirring
carefully and continuously.
Garnish with a peach ball in the
bottom of the glass, then serve.**

This cocktail has truly stood the test of time, as popular now as when it was sipped by stars of the silver screen in the 1940s. It's a simple and delicious cocktail that epitomizes the elegance and sophistication of that era and still lends that same touch of urbanity (one hopes!) to those who drink it today.

25 ml brandy
1 white sugar cube
2 dashes of Angostura bitters
dry champagne

Moisten the sugar cube with Angostura bitters and place in a champagne flute. Add the brandy, then gently pour in the champagne and serve.

champagne
cocktail

111

Two creations from the Met Bar in London were inspired by the fashion and film luvvies who always had an inexhaustible appetite for the newest champagne cocktails. The Metropolis was a logical creation since the champagne and berry-flavoured liqueur combination was such an obvious success in the Kir Royale. Adding vodka gave a kick to that same seductive mix of champagne and fruit flavours. The Ginger Champagne, highly recommended to all sushi lovers, once again uses vodka to boost its strength. The ginger combines conspiratorially with the champagne to create a cocktail that is delicate yet different enough to appease even the most sophisticated cocktail drinker.

metropolis

25 ml vodka
25 ml crème de framboise
champagne

Shake the vodka and the crème de framboise together over ice and strain into a cocktail glass. Top with champagne and serve.

ginger
champagne

25 ml vodka
2 thin slices ginger
champagne

Put the ginger in a shaker and
press with a barspoon or muddler
to release the flavour. Add ice
and the vodka, shake and strain
into a champagne flute. Top
with champagne and serve.

french 75

50 ml gin
25 ml fresh lemon juice
12.5 ml sugar syrup
champagne

Shake the gin, lemon juice and
sugar syrup over ice and strain
into a champagne flute. Top
with champagne and garnish
with a long strip of lemon zest.

james bond

The James Bond is a variation
on the Champagne Cocktail,
using vodka instead of the
more traditional brandy. The
naming of this cocktail is a
mystery to me since the
eponymous spy liked his drinks
shaken not stirred, as in this
cocktail. The French 75 is
another classic cocktail from
Harry's New York Bar in Paris.
It's not unlike a Gin Sling but
is topped up with champagne
instead of vodka.

25 ml vodka
1 white sugar cube
2 dashes of Angostura bitters
champagne

Moisten the sugar cube with
Angostura bitters and put into a
martini glass. Cover the sugar
cube with the vodka and top
with champagne.

If there is another drink in the world that looks more tempting and drinkable than a Black Velvet, then please someone, make one for me now. Pour this drink gently into the glass to allow for the somewhat unpredictable nature of both the Guinness and the champagne.

Guinness
champagne

Half fill a champagne flute with Guinness, gently top with champagne and serve.

black velvet

non-alcoholic
cocktails

There are plenty of very good reasons for drinking an alcohol-free drink, even if your friends are happily indulging in the real thing.

Driving home is obviously the most valid one; pregnancy is a good one; and being under age is a legitimate reason. The thing that scares the bejesus out of all bartenders though is being permanently on the wagon! Until recently though, little or no attention had been paid to the development of this poor relation of the cocktail world.

A perfect start to the day is the Virgin Mary (or Bloody Shame, as we bartenders call it), a meal and a drink all in one. Or, if it's a thirst quencher you're after, try a Virgin Mojito. In fact, most Collinses, Coolers and Breezes can be converted into creditable non-alcoholic beverages. It's worth experimenting on your own because it's very difficult to go too far wrong. The secret to making a really good non-alcoholic drink is to find a good balance between sweetness and acidity.

cordial
highball

25 ml cordial (of your choice)
soda water or mineral water

Pour the cordial into a highball
filled with ice and top with
either soda or mineral water.
Garnish with whatever best suits
the flavour of the cordial.

even non-alcoholic cocktails should aim for that perfect contrast of sweet and sour flavours

150 ml fresh orange juice
150 ml fresh grapefruit juice
a dash of grenadine
2 dashes of fresh lemon juice

Shake the ingredients well over ice and strain into a highball glass filled with ice.

pussy foot

Whilst researching this book, I dug out a 1935 first edition copy of the *Old Mr. Boston Bartenders' Guide*, which was once the definitive guide to mixing drinks. Luckily for us, this bible of the bar world chose to include instructions for the preparation of a lemon squash! How would Wimbledon have survived without good old Mr. Boston? It goes to show that most of us have been making cocktails all our lives without even realizing it! It's no secret that non-alcoholic cocktails are not my favourite drinks to make but they do have an important role to play in the drinks world and, as a non-alcoholic drink, the Pussy Foot ain't too bad. It fulfils all the basic criteria for this drink category – refreshing, thirst quenching and, most importantly, devoid of any alcohol – and can lead the way to a number of different juice-based drinks. Try using freshly squeezed pineapple juice instead of grapefruit for a slightly sweeter variation.

Three non-alcoholic cocktails that each serve a different purpose. The Virgin Mary is for those who feel a little worse for wear and can't face either food or alcohol. It's the perfect solution: a meal in a glass. The Shirley Temple is a thirst quencher for the very sweet-toothed and most appropriately named after the famous Hollywood child actress. The Liver Recovery is, as the name suggests, a drink that contains all the necessary goodness to restore an ailing liver without having to resort to milk thistle pills. Between them, strawberries, bananas and apples contain more nutrients and healing properties than I could fit on this page and, even better, the drink tastes great!

virgin mary

300 ml tomato juice
2 grinds of black pepper
2 dashes of Tabasco sauce
2 dashes of Worcestershire sauce
2 dashes of fresh lemon juice
1 barspoon horseradish sauce
1 celery stick

Shake all the ingredients over ice and strain into a highball filled with ice. Garnish with a celery stick. (Since this variation of the Bloody Mary is without vodka, I tend to go a bit crazy on the spices to compensate!)

shirley temple

25 ml grenadine
ginger ale or lemonade

Pour the grenadine into a glass filled with ice and top with either ginger ale or lemonade. Garnish with a slice of lemon and serve with a straw.

liver
recovery

6 fresh strawberries
2 green apples
1 banana

Peel, core, top and tail the assembled
fruits, as necessary. Put each of them
through a juicer, collecting the
resulting juice. Add the juices to a
blender filled with one scoop of
crushed ice. Blend and pour into a
small highball glass.

hangover cures

As with everything, the highs come before the lows, therefore hangover cures are an aspect of bartending that cannot be ignored – for, in a truly biblical way, what the bartender giveth so shall he taketh away.

Curing hangovers can be painless, and should be enjoyable, but there is also a lesson to be learnt, which is why the hangover cure or pick-me-up will invariably work; it will leave your taste buds a message that won't be forgotten in a hurry. The objective of a hangover cure is to get you back on that horse straight away before you spend too much time reflecting on your early morning pledge never to get in such a state again.

Different people deal with hangovers in different ways; those who lie in bed and bemoan their demise and those who strive to prepare themselves for the night ahead. The best way to prevent a hangover is to drink vast amounts of water and less alcohol but there's absolutely no fun to be had in that, so here are my alternatives. From the Prairie Oyster to the Stormy Weather, it's up to you how much penance you inflict upon yourself.

curing hangovers should be enjoyable too

bloody
mary

50 ml vodka
200 ml tomato juice
2 grinds of black pepper
2 dashes of Worcestershire sauce
2 dashes of Tabasco sauce
2 dashes of fresh lemon juice
1 barspoon horseradish sauce
1 celery stick

Shake all the ingredients over
ice and strain into a highball
glass filled with ice. Garnish
with a celery stick. (These
measurements are dependent
on personal likes or dislikes
for spices.)

corpse reviver

25 ml calvados (apple brandy)
25 ml vermouth rosso
25 ml brandy

Shake the ingredients over ice and strain into a frosted martini glass. Garnish with a slice of orange and serve.

prairie oyster

1 egg yolk
a dash of olive oil
a dashes of Tabasco sauce
2 dashes of Worcestershire sauce
salt and pepper
2 dashes of vinegar or lemon juice

Rinse a cocktail glass with the olive oil and carefully add the egg yolk. Add the seasoning to taste and serve. This cocktail is best drunk quickly in one (for obvious reasons!).

The Corpse Reviver is very much a hair-of-the-dog type of hangover cure. It will either ease your suffering completely or send you straight back to sleep. The Prairie Oyster is not for the faint-hearted but it is one of those drinks that you have to have tried at least once in your life. The Vodka Stinger gives your mouth a certain minty freshness that will at least banish any lingering night-before tastes. The Stormy Weather is well qualified to treat your hangover with its good measure of Fernet Branca, a very bitter digestif that is often used on its own as a hangover cure.

vodka
stinger

50 ml vodka
a large dash of crème de menthe
 (white)

Shake the ingredients over ice
and strain into a martini glass.

stormy
weather

25 ml Fernet Branca
25 ml dry vermouth
2 dashes of crème de menthe

Shake all the ingredients over
ice, strain into a small highball
glass filled with ice and garnish
with a sprig of mint.

index

Absinthe Cocktail, 96
Americano, 94
apple juice
    Double Vision, 34
Azure Martini, 87

Bacardi Cocktail, 76
Bellini, 110
Black Russian, 40
Black Dog, 77
Black Velvet, 115
blending, 13
Bloody Mary, 123
Blue Blazer, 68
Boston Sour, 62
bourbon:
    Boston Sour, 62
    Mint Julep, 66
    New Orleans Sazarac, 67
    Old Fashioned, 62
brandy, 88–92
    Brandy Alexander, 92
    Champagne Cocktail, 111
    Sidecar, 91
    Stinger, 90
Brazilian Mule, 30
Breakfast Martini, 26
building, 13

cachaça, 86–7
    Azure Martini, 87
    Caipirinha, 87
    Passion Fruit Batida, 87
Caipirinha, 87
calvados:
    Corpse Reviver, 124
Campari:
    Americano, 94
    Negroni, 95
    Sour Italian, 94
Chambord:
    Purple Haze, 28

champagne, 108–15
    Bellini, 110
    Black Velvet, 115
    Champagne Cocktail, 111
    French 75, 114
    Ginger Champagne, 113
    James Bond, 114
    Metropolis, 112
    Tequila Slammer, 105
champagne flutes, 15
Chocolate Mint Martini, 19
Churchill Martini, 47
cocktail glasses, 15
coffee:
    Vodka Espresso, 33
Cointreau:
    Sidecar, 91
cola:
    Cuba Libre, 84
collins glasses, 15
Conmemorativo, 103
Cordial Highball, 118
Corpse Reviver, 124
cranberry juice:
    Jamaican Breeze, 74
    Madras, 39
    Sea Breeze, 38
    Tropical Breeze, 39
Cranilla Martini, 19
crème de cacao:
    Brandy Alexander, 92
    Chocolate Mint Martini, 19
    Golden Cadillac, 99
crème de menthe:
    Grasshopper, 98
    Stinger, 90
Cuba Libre, 84
Cynar Cocktail, 93

Daiquiri, 73
Detox, 29
Dirty Martini, 46
Double Vision, 34

Drambuie:
    Rusty Nail, 62

eggs:
    Prairie Oyster, 124
equipment, 10–11

FDR Martini, 46
Fernet Branca
    Stormy Weather, 125
fraise·de bois:
    Strawberry Mule, 31
French 75, 114
fruit martinis, 20–1

Galliano:
    Harvey Wallbanger, 37
Gin Gimlet, 53
gin, 42–57
    Churchill Martini, 47
    FDR Martini, 46
    French 75, 114
    Gin Bramble, 50–1
    Gin Gimlet, 53
    Golden Bronx, 55
    The Journalist, 57
    New Orleans Fizz, 48
    Pink Gin, 52
    Royal Gin Fizz, 48
    Sapphire Martini, 44–5
    Silver Bronx, 55
    Smoky Martini, 46
ginger beer:
    Moscow Mule, 30
Ginger Champagne, 113
glasses, 14–15
Golden Bronx, 55
Golden Cadillac, 99
Grasshopper, 98
grenadine:
    Shirley Temple, 120
Guinness:
    Black Velvet, 115

hangover cures, 122–5
Harvey Wallbanger, 37
highball glasses, 15
Honey Colada, 79
Hot Toddy, 65

Jamaican Breeze, 74
James Bond, 114
The Journalist, 57

kahlúa:
    Black Russian, 40
    White Russian, 40
Kiwi Martini, 20
Krupnik Sour, 35
kummel:
    Silver Streak, 27

layering, 13
lemon juice:
    Hot Toddy, 65
    Krupnik Sour, 35
    New Orleans Fizz, 48
    Orange Daiquiri, 73
    Royal Gin Fizz, 48
    Sour Italian, 94
lime juice:
    Bacardi Cocktail, 76
    Gin Bramble, 50–1
    Original Daiquiri, 73
Liver Recovery, 121

Madras, 39
Mai Tai, 80
Manhattans, 60–1
Margarita, 102
martini glasses, 15
martinis:
    Breakfast Martini, 26
    Chocolate Mint Martini, 19
    Churchill Martini, 47
    Cranilla Martini, 19
    FDR Martini, 46

Kiwi Martini, 20
Polish Martini, 18
Sake Martini, 25
Sapphire Martini, 44–5
Smoky Martini, 46
Strawberry Martini, 20
Vodkatini, 24
Watermelon Martini, 21
measures, 11
Metropolis, 112
Metropolitan, 22–3
Mint Julep, 66
mixology techniques, 12–13
Mojito, 84
Moscow Mule, 30
muddling, 13
Mules, 30–1

Naked Martini, 47
Negroni, 95
New Orleans Fizz, 48
New Orleans Sazarac, 67
non-alcoholic cocktails, 116–21

Old Fashioned, 62
old fashioned glasses, 15
Orange Daiquiri, 73
orange juice:
    Golden Cadillac, 99
    Pussy Foot, 119
    Golden Bronx, 55
    Silver Bronx, 55

Passion Fruit Batida, 87
peach schnapps:
    Detox, 29
peaches:
    Bellini, 110
Perfect Manhattan, 61
Pernod:
    Absinthe Suissesse, 96
    New Orleans Sazarac, 67
Piña Colada, 79

pineapple juice:
    Piña Colada, 79
    Rum Runner, 75
Pink Gin, 52
Planter's Punch, 83
Polish Martini, 18
Prairie Oyster, 124
Purple Haze, 28
Pussy Foot, 119

Ramos Gin Fizz, 48
rocks glasses, 15
Royal Gin Fizz, 48
Rude Cosmopolitan, 104
rum, 70–85
    Bacardi Cocktail, 76
    Black Dog, 77
    Cuba Libre, 84
    Honey Colada, 79
    Jamaican Breeze, 74
    Mai Tai, 80
    Mojito, 84
    Orange Daiquiri, 73
    Original Daiquiri, 73
    Piña Colada, 79
    Planter's Punch, 83
    Rum Runner, 75
    T-Punch, 83
Rusty Nail, 62
rye whiskey:
    Manhattan, 60–1

Sake Martini, 25
Sangrita, 107
Sapphire Martini, 44–5
Sea Breeze, 38
shakers, 11
shaking, 13
Shirley Temple, 120
shot glasses, 15
Sidecar, 91
Silver and Golden Bronx, 55
Silver Streak, 27

Smoky Martini, 46
Sour Italian, 94
Stinger, 90
stirring, 13
Stormy Weather, 125
strawberries:
    Liver Recovery, 121
    Strawberry Martini, 20
    Strawberry Mule, 31
sugar syrup, 13

tequila, 100–7
    Conmemorativo, 103
    Margarita, 102
    Rude Cosmopolitan, 104
    Sangrita, 107
    Tequila Slammer, 105
tomato juice:
    Bloody Mary, 123
    Sangrita, 107
    Virgin Mary, 120
T-Punch, 83
triple sec:
    Conmemorativo, 103
    Margarita, 102
    Metropolitan, 22–3
    Rude Cosmopolitan, 104
Tropical Breeze, 39

vermouth:
    Americano, 94
    Churchill Martini, 47
    Corpse Reviver, 124
    Cynar Cocktail, 93
    Dry Manhattan, 61
    Negroni, 95
    Perfect Manhattan, 61
    Stormy Weather, 125
    Sweet Manhattan, 61
    Vodkatini, 24
Virgin Mary, 120
vodka, 16–41
    Black Russian, 40

Bloody Mary, 123
Brazilian Mule, 30
Breakfast Martini, 26
Chocolate Mint Martini, 19
Cranilla Martini, 19
Detox, 29
Double Vision, 34
Harvey Wallbanger, 37
Kiwi Martini, 20
Krupnik Sour, 35
Madras, 39
Metropolis, 112
Metropolitan, 22–3
Moscow Mule, 30
Polish Martini, 18
Purple Haze, 28
Sake Martini, 25
Sea Breeze, 38
Silver Streak, 27
Strawberry Martini, 20
Strawberry Mule, 31
Tropical Breeze, 39
Vodka Espresso, 33
Vodka Stinger, 125
Vodkatini, 24
Watermelon Martini, 21
White Russian, 40

Watermelon Martini, 21
whisky, 58–69
    Blue Blazer, 68
    Boston Sour, 62
    Hot Toddy, 65
    Manhattan, 60–1
    Mint Julep, 66
    New Orleans Sazarac, 67
    Old Fashioned, 62
    Rusty Nail, 62

ACKNOWLEDGEMENTS

The guidance and motivation for this book came from Anne Ryland, who despite many unreturned messages and missed deadlines managed to keep her cool (and her marbles) throughout. Many thanks to Woody's and all its staff for their patience when I was juggling more than one job (and more than one personality!). Thank you also to the Met Bar and all its mixologists for their ceaseless pursuit of the perfect martini. Thanks to Douglas at The Lab for sorting out an old mate in time of need (if you're in Soho he also makes some tasty cocktails too!). Muchas gracias to Jonny Beach for all the times you've popped up with a solution to my dilemmas. Dick Bradsell deserves recognition for flying the flag on behalf of all us bartenders. And Jasper Eyears, despite being a complete anorak, I appreciate the lesson you taught me, that attention to detail, however trivial, is always worth it. Thanks to all at *The Times* for giving me the early opportunity to voice my opinions to those that cared to listen. And nice one Bobbsy for starting out as the young Skywalker and becoming a Jedi Master. A big congrats and thank you to William Lingwood, inspired photographer, accomplished drinker and recent father.

The publisher and author would like to thank the following companies and stores who loaned the glassware, mats, bar equipment, linens and accessories that appear in the book:

The Conran Shop
81 Fulham Road
London SW3
020 7589 7401

Divertimenti
139 Fulham Road
London SW3
020 7581 8065

Heal's
196 Tottenham Court Road
London W1
020 7636 1666

Jerry's Homestore
163 Fulham Road
London SW3
020 7581 0909

Purves & Purves
83 Tottenham Court Road
London W1
020 7580 8223

We would also like to thank MyHotel Bloomsbury, for allowing us to photograph at:

Mybar
MyHotel Bloomsbury
11–13 Bayley Street
London WC1
020 7667 6000